Unit #	
Date:	
Inspected By:	

Move In Ready Checklist

Yes	No	Clean Working Light Bulb In Every Socket Including Refrigerator, Oven, Rangehood and Outside Light.
Yes	No	All light fixtures are clean inside and out, including ceiling fans.
Yes	No	Refrigerator and freezer clean, wall behind and floor underneath as well.
Yes	No	Kitchen sink, faucet, sprayer, surround and all countertops including edges and lips should be clean.
Yes	No	Dishwasher should be clean inside and out.
Yes	No	The range, burners, spill pans, inside edges of oven door, and range hood, including range fan filter and light. The floor beneath and the spaces between should be clean.
Yes	No	Kitchen backsplashes, including light and outlet switches, and undersides of all cabinets should be clean.
Yes	No	Insides of drawers, shelves, and cabinets and exterior cabinet doors as well as countertops.
Yes	No	Bathroom toilets inside/outside, faucets, bathtubs, showers, mirrors and bathroom fans.
Yes	No	Woodwork, trim, baseboards, thermostats, vents, heaters, light switches, outlets, smoke and CO2 detectors, doorbell boxes should all be clean.
Yes	No	Windows inside and out and tracks should be clean.
Yes	No	Hardwood floors and baseboards.
Yes	No	Carpets are stain and damage free
Yes	No	Walls, doors, ceilings are clean and damage free.
Yes	No	Washing/Drying Machine including dryer seal as well as laundry floor and drains.
Yes	No	Garage is clean including walls, floors, and fixtures.

I0402823

Tenant(s) Signature:	**Date:**
Property Administrator Signature:	**Date:**

Unit #	
Date:	
Inspected By:	

Move In Ready Checklist

Yes	No	Clean Working Light Bulb In Every Socket Including Refrigerator, Oven, Rangehood and Outside Light.
Yes	No	All light fixtures are clean inside and out, including ceiling fans.
Yes	No	Refrigerator and freezer clean, wall behind and floor underneath as well.
Yes	No	Kitchen sink, faucet, sprayer, surround and all countertops including edges and lips should be clean.
Yes	No	Dishwasher should be clean inside and out.
Yes	No	The range, burners, spill pans, inside edges of oven door, and range hood, including range fan filter and light. The floor beneath and the spaces between should be clean.
Yes	No	Kitchen backsplashes, including light and outlet switches, and undersides of all cabinets should be clean.
Yes	No	Insides of drawers, shelves, and cabinets and exterior cabinet doors as well as countertops.
Yes	No	Bathroom toilets inside/outside, faucets, bathtubs, showers, mirrors and bathroom fans.
Yes	No	Woodwork, trim, baseboards, thermostats, vents, heaters, light switches, outlets, smoke and CO2 detectors, doorbell boxes should all be clean.
Yes	No	Windows inside and out and tracks should be clean.
Yes	No	Hardwood floors and baseboards.
Yes	No	Carpets are stain and damage free
Yes	No	Walls, doors, ceilings are clean and damage free.
Yes	No	Washing/Drying Machine including dryer seal as well as laundry floor and drains.
Yes	No	Garage is clean including walls, floors, and fixtures.

Tenant(s) Signature:	**Date:**
Property Administrator Signature:	**Date:**

Unit #	
Date:	
Inspected By:	

Move In Ready Checklist

Yes	No	Clean Working Light Bulb In Every Socket Including Refrigerator, Oven, Rangehood and Outside Light.
Yes	No	All light fixtures are clean inside and out, including ceiling fans.
Yes	No	Refrigerator and freezer clean, wall behind and floor underneath as well.
Yes	No	Kitchen sink, faucet, sprayer, surround and all countertops including edges and lips should be clean.
Yes	No	Dishwasher should be clean inside and out.
Yes	No	The range, burners, spill pans, inside edges of oven door, and range hood, including range fan filter and light. The floor beneath and the spaces between should be clean.
Yes	No	Kitchen backsplashes, including light and outlet switches, and undersides of all cabinets should be clean.
Yes	No	Insides of drawers, shelves, and cabinets and exterior cabinet doors as well as countertops.
Yes	No	Bathroom toilets inside/outside, faucets, bathtubs, showers, mirrors and bathroom fans.
Yes	No	Woodwork, trim, baseboards, thermostats, vents, heaters, light switches, outlets, smoke and CO2 detectors, doorbell boxes should all be clean.
Yes	No	Windows inside and out and tracks should be clean.
Yes	No	Hardwood floors and baseboards.
Yes	No	Carpets are stain and damage free
Yes	No	Walls, doors, ceilings are clean and damage free.
Yes	No	Washing/Drying Machine including dryer seal as well as laundry floor and drains.
Yes	No	Garage is clean including walls, floors, and fixtures.

Tenant(s) Signature:	**Date:**
Property Administrator Signature:	**Date:**

Unit #	
Date:	
Inspected By:	

Move In Ready Checklist

Yes	No	Clean Working Light Bulb In Every Socket Including Refrigerator, Oven, Rangehood and Outside Light.
Yes	No	All light fixtures are clean inside and out, including ceiling fans.
Yes	No	Refrigerator and freezer clean, wall behind and floor underneath as well.
Yes	No	Kitchen sink, faucet, sprayer, surround and all countertops including edges and lips should be clean.
Yes	No	Dishwasher should be clean inside and out.
Yes	No	The range, burners, spill pans, inside edges of oven door, and range hood, including range fan filter and light. The floor beneath and the spaces between should be clean.
Yes	No	Kitchen backsplashes, including light and outlet switches, and undersides of all cabinets should be clean.
Yes	No	Insides of drawers, shelves, and cabinets and exterior cabinet doors as well as countertops.
Yes	No	Bathroom toilets inside/outside, faucets, bathtubs, showers, mirrors and bathroom fans.
Yes	No	Woodwork, trim, baseboards, thermostats, vents, heaters, light switches, outlets, smoke and CO2 detectors, doorbell boxes should all be clean.
Yes	No	Windows inside and out and tracks should be clean.
Yes	No	Hardwood floors and baseboards.
Yes	No	Carpets are stain and damage free
Yes	No	Walls, doors, ceilings are clean and damage free.
Yes	No	Washing/Drying Machine including dryer seal as well as laundry floor and drains.
Yes	No	Garage is clean including walls, floors, and fixtures.

Tenant(s) Signature:	**Date:**
Property Administrator Signature:	**Date:**

Unit #		
Date:		
Inspected By:		

Move In Ready Checklist

Yes	No	Clean Working Light Bulb In Every Socket Including Refrigerator, Oven, Rangehood and Outside Light.
Yes	No	All light fixtures are clean inside and out, including ceiling fans.
Yes	No	Refrigerator and freezer clean, wall behind and floor underneath as well.
Yes	No	Kitchen sink, faucet, sprayer, surround and all countertops including edges and lips should be clean.
Yes	No	Dishwasher should be clean inside and out.
Yes	No	The range, burners, spill pans, inside edges of oven door, and range hood, including range fan filter and light. The floor beneath and the spaces between should be clean.
Yes	No	Kitchen backsplashes, including light and outlet switches, and undersides of all cabinets should be clean.
Yes	No	Insides of drawers, shelves, and cabinets and exterior cabinet doors as well as countertops.
Yes	No	Bathroom toilets inside/outside, faucets, bathtubs, showers, mirrors and bathroom fans.
Yes	No	Woodwork, trim, baseboards, thermostats, vents, heaters, light switches, outlets, smoke and CO2 detectors, doorbell boxes should all be clean.
Yes	No	Windows inside and out and tracks should be clean.
Yes	No	Hardwood floors and baseboards.
Yes	No	Carpets are stain and damage free
Yes	No	Walls, doors, ceilings are clean and damage free.
Yes	No	Washing/Drying Machine including dryer seal as well as laundry floor and drains.
Yes	No	Garage is clean including walls, floors, and fixtures.

Tenant(s) Signature:	**Date:**
Property Administrator Signature:	**Date:**

Unit #	
Date:	
Inspected By:	

Move In Ready Checklist

Yes	No	Clean Working Light Bulb In Every Socket Including Refrigerator, Oven, Rangehood and Outside Light.
Yes	No	All light fixtures are clean inside and out, including ceiling fans.
Yes	No	Refrigerator and freezer clean, wall behind and floor underneath as well.
Yes	No	Kitchen sink, faucet, sprayer, surround and all countertops including edges and lips should be clean.
Yes	No	Dishwasher should be clean inside and out.
Yes	No	The range, burners, spill pans, inside edges of oven door, and range hood, including range fan filter and light. The floor beneath and the spaces between should be clean.
Yes	No	Kitchen backsplashes, including light and outlet switches, and undersides of all cabinets should be clean.
Yes	No	Insides of drawers, shelves, and cabinets and exterior cabinet doors as well as countertops.
Yes	No	Bathroom toilets inside/outside, faucets, bathtubs, showers, mirrors and bathroom fans.
Yes	No	Woodwork, trim, baseboards, thermostats, vents, heaters, light switches, outlets, smoke and CO2 detectors, doorbell boxes should all be clean.
Yes	No	Windows inside and out and tracks should be clean.
Yes	No	Hardwood floors and baseboards.
Yes	No	Carpets are stain and damage free
Yes	No	Walls, doors, ceilings are clean and damage free.
Yes	No	Washing/Drying Machine including dryer seal as well as laundry floor and drains.
Yes	No	Garage is clean including walls, floors, and fixtures.

Tenant(s) Signature:	**Date:**
Property Administrator Signature:	**Date:**

Unit #	
Date:	
Inspected By:	

Move In Ready Checklist

Yes	No	Clean Working Light Bulb In Every Socket Including Refrigerator, Oven, Rangehood and Outside Light.
Yes	No	All light fixtures are clean inside and out, including ceiling fans.
Yes	No	Refrigerator and freezer clean, wall behind and floor underneath as well.
Yes	No	Kitchen sink, faucet, sprayer, surround and all countertops including edges and lips should be clean.
Yes	No	Dishwasher should be clean inside and out.
Yes	No	The range, burners, spill pans, inside edges of oven door, and range hood, including range fan filter and light. The floor beneath and the spaces between should be clean.
Yes	No	Kitchen backsplashes, including light and outlet switches, and undersides of all cabinets should be clean.
Yes	No	Insides of drawers, shelves, and cabinets and exterior cabinet doors as well as countertops.
Yes	No	Bathroom toilets inside/outside, faucets, bathtubs, showers, mirrors and bathroom fans.
Yes	No	Woodwork, trim, baseboards, thermostats, vents, heaters, light switches, outlets, smoke and CO2 detectors, doorbell boxes should all be clean.
Yes	No	Windows inside and out and tracks should be clean.
Yes	No	Hardwood floors and baseboards.
Yes	No	Carpets are stain and damage free
Yes	No	Walls, doors, ceilings are clean and damage free.
Yes	No	Washing/Drying Machine including dryer seal as well as laundry floor and drains.
Yes	No	Garage is clean including walls, floors, and fixtures.

Tenant(s) Signature:	**Date:**
Property Administrator Signature:	**Date:**

Unit #	
Date:	
Inspected By:	

Move In Ready Checklist

Yes	No	Clean Working Light Bulb In Every Socket Including Refrigerator, Oven, Rangehood and Outside Light.
Yes	No	All light fixtures are clean inside and out, including ceiling fans.
Yes	No	Refrigerator and freezer clean, wall behind and floor underneath as well.
Yes	No	Kitchen sink, faucet, sprayer, surround and all countertops including edges and lips should be clean.
Yes	No	Dishwasher should be clean inside and out.
Yes	No	The range, burners, spill pans, inside edges of oven door, and range hood, including range fan filter and light. The floor beneath and the spaces between should be clean.
Yes	No	Kitchen backsplashes, including light and outlet switches, and undersides of all cabinets should be clean.
Yes	No	Insides of drawers, shelves, and cabinets and exterior cabinet doors as well as countertops.
Yes	No	Bathroom toilets inside/outside, faucets, bathtubs, showers, mirrors and bathroom fans.
Yes	No	Woodwork, trim, baseboards, thermostats, vents, heaters, light switches, outlets, smoke and CO2 detectors, doorbell boxes should all be clean.
Yes	No	Windows inside and out and tracks should be clean.
Yes	No	Hardwood floors and baseboards.
Yes	No	Carpets are stain and damage free
Yes	No	Walls, doors, ceilings are clean and damage free.
Yes	No	Washing/Drying Machine including dryer seal as well as laundry floor and drains.
Yes	No	Garage is clean including walls, floors, and fixtures.

Tenant(s) Signature:	**Date:**
Property Administrator Signature:	**Date:**

Unit #	
Date:	
Inspected By:	

Move In Ready Checklist

Yes	No	Clean Working Light Bulb In Every Socket Including Refrigerator, Oven, Rangehood and Outside Light.
Yes	No	All light fixtures are clean inside and out, including ceiling fans.
Yes	No	Refrigerator and freezer clean, wall behind and floor underneath as well.
Yes	No	Kitchen sink, faucet, sprayer, surround and all countertops including edges and lips should be clean.
Yes	No	Dishwasher should be clean inside and out.
Yes	No	The range, burners, spill pans, inside edges of oven door, and range hood, including range fan filter and light. The floor beneath and the spaces between should be clean.
Yes	No	Kitchen backsplashes, including light and outlet switches, and undersides of all cabinets should be clean.
Yes	No	Insides of drawers, shelves, and cabinets and exterior cabinet doors as well as countertops.
Yes	No	Bathroom toilets inside/outside, faucets, bathtubs, showers, mirrors and bathroom fans.
Yes	No	Woodwork, trim, baseboards, thermostats, vents, heaters, light switches, outlets, smoke and CO2 detectors, doorbell boxes should all be clean.
Yes	No	Windows inside and out and tracks should be clean.
Yes	No	Hardwood floors and baseboards.
Yes	No	Carpets are stain and damage free
Yes	No	Walls, doors, ceilings are clean and damage free.
Yes	No	Washing/Drying Machine including dryer seal as well as laundry floor and drains.
Yes	No	Garage is clean including walls, floors, and fixtures.

Tenant(s) Signature:	**Date:**
Property Administrator Signature:	**Date:**

Unit #	
Date:	
Inspected By:	

Move In Ready Checklist

Yes	No	Clean Working Light Bulb In Every Socket Including Refrigerator, Oven, Rangehood and Outside Light.
Yes	No	All light fixtures are clean inside and out, including ceiling fans.
Yes	No	Refrigerator and freezer clean, wall behind and floor underneath as well.
Yes	No	Kitchen sink, faucet, sprayer, surround and all countertops including edges and lips should be clean.
Yes	No	Dishwasher should be clean inside and out.
Yes	No	The range, burners, spill pans, inside edges of oven door, and range hood, including range fan filter and light. The floor beneath and the spaces between should be clean.
Yes	No	Kitchen backsplashes, including light and outlet switches, and undersides of all cabinets should be clean.
Yes	No	Insides of drawers, shelves, and cabinets and exterior cabinet doors as well as countertops.
Yes	No	Bathroom toilets inside/outside, faucets, bathtubs, showers, mirrors and bathroom fans.
Yes	No	Woodwork, trim, baseboards, thermostats, vents, heaters, light switches, outlets, smoke and CO2 detectors, doorbell boxes should all be clean.
Yes	No	Windows inside and out and tracks should be clean.
Yes	No	Hardwood floors and baseboards.
Yes	No	Carpets are stain and damage free
Yes	No	Walls, doors, ceilings are clean and damage free.
Yes	No	Washing/Drying Machine including dryer seal as well as laundry floor and drains.
Yes	No	Garage is clean including walls, floors, and fixtures.

Tenant(s) Signature:	**Date:**
Property Administrator Signature:	**Date:**

Unit #:	
Date:	
Inspected By:	

Move In Ready Checklist

Yes	No	Clean Working Light Bulb In Every Socket Including Refrigerator, Oven, Rangehood and Outside Light.
Yes	No	All light fixtures are clean inside and out, including ceiling fans.
Yes	No	Refrigerator and freezer clean, wall behind and floor underneath as well.
Yes	No	Kitchen sink, faucet, sprayer, surround and all countertops including edges and lips should be clean.
Yes	No	Dishwasher should be clean inside and out.
Yes	No	The range, burners, spill pans, inside edges of oven door, and range hood, including range fan filter and light. The floor beneath and the spaces between should be clean.
Yes	No	Kitchen backsplashes, including light and outlet switches, and undersides of all cabinets should be clean.
Yes	No	Insides of drawers, shelves, and cabinets and exterior cabinet doors as well as countertops.
Yes	No	Bathroom toilets inside/outside, faucets, bathtubs, showers, mirrors and bathroom fans.
Yes	No	Woodwork, trim, baseboards, thermostats, vents, heaters, light switches, outlets, smoke and CO2 detectors, doorbell boxes should all be clean.
Yes	No	Windows inside and out and tracks should be clean.
Yes	No	Hardwood floors and baseboards.
Yes	No	Carpets are stain and damage free
Yes	No	Walls, doors, ceilings are clean and damage free.
Yes	No	Washing/Drying Machine including dryer seal as well as laundry floor and drains.
Yes	No	Garage is clean including walls, floors, and fixtures.

Tenant(s) Signature: **Date:**

Property Administrator Signature: **Date:**

Unit #	
Date:	
Inspected By:	

Move In Ready Checklist

Yes	No	Clean Working Light Bulb In Every Socket Including Refrigerator, Oven, Rangehood and Outside Light.
Yes	No	All light fixtures are clean inside and out, including ceiling fans.
Yes	No	Refrigerator and freezer clean, wall behind and floor underneath as well.
Yes	No	Kitchen sink, faucet, sprayer, surround and all countertops including edges and lips should be clean.
Yes	No	Dishwasher should be clean inside and out.
Yes	No	The range, burners, spill pans, inside edges of oven door, and range hood, including range fan filter and light. The floor beneath and the spaces between should be clean.
Yes	No	Kitchen backsplashes, including light and outlet switches, and undersides of all cabinets should be clean.
Yes	No	Insides of drawers, shelves, and cabinets and exterior cabinet doors as well as countertops.
Yes	No	Bathroom toilets inside/outside, faucets, bathtubs, showers, mirrors and bathroom fans.
Yes	No	Woodwork, trim, baseboards, thermostats, vents, heaters, light switches, outlets, smoke and CO2 detectors, doorbell boxes should all be clean.
Yes	No	Windows inside and out and tracks should be clean.
Yes	No	Hardwood floors and baseboards.
Yes	No	Carpets are stain and damage free
Yes	No	Walls, doors, ceilings are clean and damage free.
Yes	No	Washing/Drying Machine including dryer seal as well as laundry floor and drains.
Yes	No	Garage is clean including walls, floors, and fixtures.

Tenant(s) Signature:	**Date:**
Property Administrator Signature:	**Date:**

Unit #		
Date:		
Inspected By:		

Move In Ready Checklist

Yes	No	Clean Working Light Bulb In Every Socket Including Refrigerator, Oven, Rangehood and Outside Light.
Yes	No	All light fixtures are clean inside and out, including ceiling fans.
Yes	No	Refrigerator and freezer clean, wall behind and floor underneath as well.
Yes	No	Kitchen sink, faucet, sprayer, surround and all countertops including edges and lips should be clean.
Yes	No	Dishwasher should be clean inside and out.
Yes	No	The range, burners, spill pans, inside edges of oven door, and range hood, including range fan filter and light. The floor beneath and the spaces between should be clean.
Yes	No	Kitchen backsplashes, including light and outlet switches, and undersides of all cabinets should be clean.
Yes	No	Insides of drawers, shelves, and cabinets and exterior cabinet doors as well as countertops.
Yes	No	Bathroom toilets inside/outside, faucets, bathtubs, showers, mirrors and bathroom fans.
Yes	No	Woodwork, trim, baseboards, thermostats, vents, heaters, light switches, outlets, smoke and CO2 detectors, doorbell boxes should all be clean.
Yes	No	Windows inside and out and tracks should be clean.
Yes	No	Hardwood floors and baseboards.
Yes	No	Carpets are stain and damage free
Yes	No	Walls, doors, ceilings are clean and damage free.
Yes	No	Washing/Drying Machine including dryer seal as well as laundry floor and drains.
Yes	No	Garage is clean including walls, floors, and fixtures.

Tenant(s) Signature:	**Date:**
Property Administrator Signature:	**Date:**

Unit #	
Date:	
Inspected By:	

Move In Ready Checklist

Yes	No	Clean Working Light Bulb In Every Socket Including Refrigerator, Oven, Rangehood and Outside Light.
Yes	No	All light fixtures are clean inside and out, including ceiling fans.
Yes	No	Refrigerator and freezer clean, wall behind and floor underneath as well.
Yes	No	Kitchen sink, faucet, sprayer, surround and all countertops including edges and lips should be clean.
Yes	No	Dishwasher should be clean inside and out.
Yes	No	The range, burners, spill pans, inside edges of oven door, and range hood, including range fan filter and light. The floor beneath and the spaces between should be clean.
Yes	No	Kitchen backsplashes, including light and outlet switches, and undersides of all cabinets should be clean.
Yes	No	Insides of drawers, shelves, and cabinets and exterior cabinet doors as well as countertops.
Yes	No	Bathroom toilets inside/outside, faucets, bathtubs, showers, mirrors and bathroom fans.
Yes	No	Woodwork, trim, baseboards, thermostats, vents, heaters, light switches, outlets, smoke and CO2 detectors, doorbell boxes should all be clean.
Yes	No	Windows inside and out and tracks should be clean.
Yes	No	Hardwood floors and baseboards.
Yes	No	Carpets are stain and damage free
Yes	No	Walls, doors, ceilings are clean and damage free.
Yes	No	Washing/Drying Machine including dryer seal as well as laundry floor and drains.
Yes	No	Garage is clean including walls, floors, and fixtures.

Tenant(s) Signature:	**Date:**
Property Administrator Signature:	**Date:**

Unit #	
Date:	
Inspected By:	

Move In Ready Checklist

Yes	No	Clean Working Light Bulb In Every Socket Including Refrigerator, Oven, Rangehood and Outside Light.
Yes	No	All light fixtures are clean inside and out, including ceiling fans.
Yes	No	Refrigerator and freezer clean, wall behind and floor underneath as well.
Yes	No	Kitchen sink, faucet, sprayer, surround and all countertops including edges and lips should be clean.
Yes	No	Dishwasher should be clean inside and out.
Yes	No	The range, burners, spill pans, inside edges of oven door, and range hood, including range fan filter and light. The floor beneath and the spaces between should be clean.
Yes	No	Kitchen backsplashes, including light and outlet switches, and undersides of all cabinets should be clean.
Yes	No	Insides of drawers, shelves, and cabinets and exterior cabinet doors as well as countertops.
Yes	No	Bathroom toilets inside/outside, faucets, bathtubs, showers, mirrors and bathroom fans.
Yes	No	Woodwork, trim, baseboards, thermostats, vents, heaters, light switches, outlets, smoke and CO2 detectors, doorbell boxes should all be clean.
Yes	No	Windows inside and out and tracks should be clean.
Yes	No	Hardwood floors and baseboards.
Yes	No	Carpets are stain and damage free
Yes	No	Walls, doors, ceilings are clean and damage free.
Yes	No	Washing/Drying Machine including dryer seal as well as laundry floor and drains.
Yes	No	Garage is clean including walls, floors, and fixtures.

Tenant(s) Signature:	**Date:**
Property Administrator Signature:	**Date:**

Unit #	
Date:	
Inspected By:	

Move In Ready Checklist

Yes	No	Clean Working Light Bulb In Every Socket Including Refrigerator, Oven, Rangehood and Outside Light.
Yes	No	All light fixtures are clean inside and out, including ceiling fans.
Yes	No	Refrigerator and freezer clean, wall behind and floor underneath as well.
Yes	No	Kitchen sink, faucet, sprayer, surround and all countertops including edges and lips should be clean.
Yes	No	Dishwasher should be clean inside and out.
Yes	No	The range, burners, spill pans, inside edges of oven door, and range hood, including range fan filter and light. The floor beneath and the spaces between should be clean.
Yes	No	Kitchen backsplashes, including light and outlet switches, and undersides of all cabinets should be clean.
Yes	No	Insides of drawers, shelves, and cabinets and exterior cabinet doors as well as countertops.
Yes	No	Bathroom toilets inside/outside, faucets, bathtubs, showers, mirrors and bathroom fans.
Yes	No	Woodwork, trim, baseboards, thermostats, vents, heaters, light switches, outlets, smoke and CO2 detectors, doorbell boxes should all be clean.
Yes	No	Windows inside and out and tracks should be clean.
Yes	No	Hardwood floors and baseboards.
Yes	No	Carpets are stain and damage free
Yes	No	Walls, doors, ceilings are clean and damage free.
Yes	No	Washing/Drying Machine including dryer seal as well as laundry floor and drains.
Yes	No	Garage is clean including walls, floors, and fixtures.

Tenant(s) Signature:	**Date:**
Property Administrator Signature:	**Date:**

Unit #		
Date:		
Inspected By:		

Move In Ready Checklist

Yes	No	Clean Working Light Bulb In Every Socket Including Refrigerator, Oven, Rangehood and Outside Light.
Yes	No	All light fixtures are clean inside and out, including ceiling fans.
Yes	No	Refrigerator and freezer clean, wall behind and floor underneath as well.
Yes	No	Kitchen sink, faucet, sprayer, surround and all countertops including edges and lips should be clean.
Yes	No	Dishwasher should be clean inside and out.
Yes	No	The range, burners, spill pans, inside edges of oven door, and range hood, including range fan filter and light. The floor beneath and the spaces between should be clean.
Yes	No	Kitchen backsplashes, including light and outlet switches, and undersides of all cabinets should be clean.
Yes	No	Insides of drawers, shelves, and cabinets and exterior cabinet doors as well as countertops.
Yes	No	Bathroom toilets inside/outside, faucets, bathtubs, showers, mirrors and bathroom fans.
Yes	No	Woodwork, trim, baseboards, thermostats, vents, heaters, light switches, outlets, smoke and CO2 detectors, doorbell boxes should all be clean.
Yes	No	Windows inside and out and tracks should be clean.
Yes	No	Hardwood floors and baseboards.
Yes	No	Carpets are stain and damage free
Yes	No	Walls, doors, ceilings are clean and damage free.
Yes	No	Washing/Drying Machine including dryer seal as well as laundry floor and drains.
Yes	No	Garage is clean including walls, floors, and fixtures.

Tenant(s) Signature:	**Date:**
Property Administrator Signature:	**Date:**

Unit #	
Date:	
Inspected By:	

Move In Ready Checklist

Yes	No		Clean Working Light Bulb In Every Socket Including Refrigerator, Oven, Rangehood and Outside Light.
Yes	No		All light fixtures are clean inside and out, including ceiling fans.
Yes	No		Refrigerator and freezer clean, wall behind and floor underneath as well.
Yes	No		Kitchen sink, faucet, sprayer, surround and all countertops including edges and lips should be clean.
Yes	No		Dishwasher should be clean inside and out.
Yes	No		The range, burners, spill pans, inside edges of oven door, and range hood, including range fan filter and light. The floor beneath and the spaces between should be clean.
Yes	No		Kitchen backsplashes, including light and outlet switches, and undersides of all cabinets should be clean.
Yes	No		Insides of drawers, shelves, and cabinets and exterior cabinet doors as well as countertops.
Yes	No		Bathroom toilets inside/outside, faucets, bathtubs, showers, mirrors and bathroom fans.
Yes	No		Woodwork, trim, baseboards, thermostats, vents, heaters, light switches, outlets, smoke and CO2 detectors, doorbell boxes should all be clean.
Yes	No		Windows inside and out and tracks should be clean.
Yes	No		Hardwood floors and baseboards.
Yes	No		Carpets are stain and damage free
Yes	No		Walls, doors, ceilings are clean and damage free.
Yes	No		Washing/Drying Machine including dryer seal as well as laundry floor and drains.
Yes	No		Garage is clean including walls, floors, and fixtures.

Tenant(s) Signature:		**Date:**	
Property Administrator Signature:		**Date:**	

Unit #	
Date:	
Inspected By:	

Move In Ready Checklist

Yes	No	Clean Working Light Bulb In Every Socket Including Refrigerator, Oven, Rangehood and Outside Light.
Yes	No	All light fixtures are clean inside and out, including ceiling fans.
Yes	No	Refrigerator and freezer clean, wall behind and floor underneath as well.
Yes	No	Kitchen sink, faucet, sprayer, surround and all countertops including edges and lips should be clean.
Yes	No	Dishwasher should be clean inside and out.
Yes	No	The range, burners, spill pans, inside edges of oven door, and range hood, including range fan filter and light. The floor beneath and the spaces between should be clean.
Yes	No	Kitchen backsplashes, including light and outlet switches, and undersides of all cabinets should be clean.
Yes	No	Insides of drawers, shelves, and cabinets and exterior cabinet doors as well as countertops.
Yes	No	Bathroom toilets inside/outside, faucets, bathtubs, showers, mirrors and bathroom fans.
Yes	No	Woodwork, trim, baseboards, thermostats, vents, heaters, light switches, outlets, smoke and CO2 detectors, doorbell boxes should all be clean.
Yes	No	Windows inside and out and tracks should be clean.
Yes	No	Hardwood floors and baseboards.
Yes	No	Carpets are stain and damage free
Yes	No	Walls, doors, ceilings are clean and damage free.
Yes	No	Washing/Drying Machine including dryer seal as well as laundry floor and drains.
Yes	No	Garage is clean including walls, floors, and fixtures.

Tenant(s) Signature:	**Date:**
Property Administrator Signature:	**Date:**

Unit #	
Date:	
Inspected By:	

Move In Ready Checklist

Yes	No	Clean Working Light Bulb In Every Socket Including Refrigerator, Oven, Rangehood and Outside Light.
Yes	No	All light fixtures are clean inside and out, including ceiling fans.
Yes	No	Refrigerator and freezer clean, wall behind and floor underneath as well.
Yes	No	Kitchen sink, faucet, sprayer, surround and all countertops including edges and lips should be clean.
Yes	No	Dishwasher should be clean inside and out.
Yes	No	The range, burners, spill pans, inside edges of oven door, and range hood, including range fan filter and light. The floor beneath and the spaces between should be clean.
Yes	No	Kitchen backsplashes, including light and outlet switches, and undersides of all cabinets should be clean.
Yes	No	Insides of drawers, shelves, and cabinets and exterior cabinet doors as well as countertops.
Yes	No	Bathroom toilets inside/outside, faucets, bathtubs, showers, mirrors and bathroom fans.
Yes	No	Woodwork, trim, baseboards, thermostats, vents, heaters, light switches, outlets, smoke and CO2 detectors, doorbell boxes should all be clean.
Yes	No	Windows inside and out and tracks should be clean.
Yes	No	Hardwood floors and baseboards.
Yes	No	Carpets are stain and damage free
Yes	No	Walls, doors, ceilings are clean and damage free.
Yes	No	Washing/Drying Machine including dryer seal as well as laundry floor and drains.
Yes	No	Garage is clean including walls, floors, and fixtures.

Tenant(s) Signature:	**Date:**
Property Administrator Signature:	**Date:**

Unit #	
Date:	
Inspected By:	

Move In Ready Checklist

Yes	No	Clean Working Light Bulb In Every Socket Including Refrigerator, Oven, Rangehood and Outside Light.
Yes	No	All light fixtures are clean inside and out, including ceiling fans.
Yes	No	Refrigerator and freezer clean, wall behind and floor underneath as well.
Yes	No	Kitchen sink, faucet, sprayer, surround and all countertops including edges and lips should be clean.
Yes	No	Dishwasher should be clean inside and out.
Yes	No	The range, burners, spill pans, inside edges of oven door, and range hood, including range fan filter and light. The floor beneath and the spaces between should be clean.
Yes	No	Kitchen backsplashes, including light and outlet switches, and undersides of all cabinets should be clean.
Yes	No	Insides of drawers, shelves, and cabinets and exterior cabinet doors as well as countertops.
Yes	No	Bathroom toilets inside/outside, faucets, bathtubs, showers, mirrors and bathroom fans.
Yes	No	Woodwork, trim, baseboards, thermostats, vents, heaters, light switches, outlets, smoke and CO2 detectors, doorbell boxes should all be clean.
Yes	No	Windows inside and out and tracks should be clean.
Yes	No	Hardwood floors and baseboards.
Yes	No	Carpets are stain and damage free
Yes	No	Walls, doors, ceilings are clean and damage free.
Yes	No	Washing/Drying Machine including dryer seal as well as laundry floor and drains.
Yes	No	Garage is clean including walls, floors, and fixtures.

Tenant(s) Signature:	**Date:**
Property Administrator Signature:	**Date:**

Unit #:	
Date:	
Inspected By:	

Move In Ready Checklist

Yes	No	Clean Working Light Bulb In Every Socket Including Refrigerator, Oven, Rangehood and Outside Light.
Yes	No	All light fixtures are clean inside and out, including ceiling fans.
Yes	No	Refrigerator and freezer clean, wall behind and floor underneath as well.
Yes	No	Kitchen sink, faucet, sprayer, surround and all countertops including edges and lips should be clean.
Yes	No	Dishwasher should be clean inside and out.
Yes	No	The range, burners, spill pans, inside edges of oven door, and range hood, including range fan filter and light. The floor beneath and the spaces between should be clean.
Yes	No	Kitchen backsplashes, including light and outlet switches, and undersides of all cabinets should be clean.
Yes	No	Insides of drawers, shelves, and cabinets and exterior cabinet doors as well as countertops.
Yes	No	Bathroom toilets inside/outside, faucets, bathtubs, showers, mirrors and bathroom fans.
Yes	No	Woodwork, trim, baseboards, thermostats, vents, heaters, light switches, outlets, smoke and CO2 detectors, doorbell boxes should all be clean.
Yes	No	Windows inside and out and tracks should be clean.
Yes	No	Hardwood floors and baseboards.
Yes	No	Carpets are stain and damage free
Yes	No	Walls, doors, ceilings are clean and damage free.
Yes	No	Washing/Drying Machine including dryer seal as well as laundry floor and drains.
Yes	No	Garage is clean including walls, floors, and fixtures.

Tenant(s) Signature:	**Date:**
Property Administrator Signature:	**Date:**

Unit #	
Date:	
Inspected By:	

Move In Ready Checklist

Yes	No	Clean Working Light Bulb In Every Socket Including Refrigerator, Oven, Rangehood and Outside Light.
Yes	No	All light fixtures are clean inside and out, including ceiling fans.
Yes	No	Refrigerator and freezer clean, wall behind and floor underneath as well.
Yes	No	Kitchen sink, faucet, sprayer, surround and all countertops including edges and lips should be clean.
Yes	No	Dishwasher should be clean inside and out.
Yes	No	The range, burners, spill pans, inside edges of oven door, and range hood, including range fan filter and light. The floor beneath and the spaces between should be clean.
Yes	No	Kitchen backsplashes, including light and outlet switches, and undersides of all cabinets should be clean.
Yes	No	Insides of drawers, shelves, and cabinets and exterior cabinet doors as well as countertops.
Yes	No	Bathroom toilets inside/outside, faucets, bathtubs, showers, mirrors and bathroom fans.
Yes	No	Woodwork, trim, baseboards, thermostats, vents, heaters, light switches, outlets, smoke and CO2 detectors, doorbell boxes should all be clean.
Yes	No	Windows inside and out and tracks should be clean.
Yes	No	Hardwood floors and baseboards.
Yes	No	Carpets are stain and damage free
Yes	No	Walls, doors, ceilings are clean and damage free.
Yes	No	Washing/Drying Machine including dryer seal as well as laundry floor and drains.
Yes	No	Garage is clean including walls, floors, and fixtures.

Tenant(s) Signature:	**Date:**
Property Administrator Signature:	**Date:**

Unit #	
Date:	
Inspected By:	

Move In Ready Checklist

Yes	No	Clean Working Light Bulb In Every Socket Including Refrigerator, Oven, Rangehood and Outside Light.
Yes	No	All light fixtures are clean inside and out, including ceiling fans.
Yes	No	Refrigerator and freezer clean, wall behind and floor underneath as well.
Yes	No	Kitchen sink, faucet, sprayer, surround and all countertops including edges and lips should be clean.
Yes	No	Dishwasher should be clean inside and out.
Yes	No	The range, burners, spill pans, inside edges of oven door, and range hood, including range fan filter and light. The floor beneath and the spaces between should be clean.
Yes	No	Kitchen backsplashes, including light and outlet switches, and undersides of all cabinets should be clean.
Yes	No	Insides of drawers, shelves, and cabinets and exterior cabinet doors as well as countertops.
Yes	No	Bathroom toilets inside/outside, faucets, bathtubs, showers, mirrors and bathroom fans.
Yes	No	Woodwork, trim, baseboards, thermostats, vents, heaters, light switches, outlets, smoke and CO2 detectors, doorbell boxes should all be clean.
Yes	No	Windows inside and out and tracks should be clean.
Yes	No	Hardwood floors and baseboards.
Yes	No	Carpets are stain and damage free
Yes	No	Walls, doors, ceilings are clean and damage free.
Yes	No	Washing/Drying Machine including dryer seal as well as laundry floor and drains.
Yes	No	Garage is clean including walls, floors, and fixtures.

Tenant(s) Signature:	**Date:**
Property Administrator Signature:	**Date:**

Unit #	
Date:	
Inspected By:	

Move In Ready Checklist

Yes	No	Clean Working Light Bulb In Every Socket Including Refrigerator, Oven, Rangehood and Outside Light.
Yes	No	All light fixtures are clean inside and out, including ceiling fans.
Yes	No	Refrigerator and freezer clean, wall behind and floor underneath as well.
Yes	No	Kitchen sink, faucet, sprayer, surround and all countertops including edges and lips should be clean.
Yes	No	Dishwasher should be clean inside and out.
Yes	No	The range, burners, spill pans, inside edges of oven door, and range hood, including range fan filter and light. The floor beneath and the spaces between should be clean.
Yes	No	Kitchen backsplashes, including light and outlet switches, and undersides of all cabinets should be clean.
Yes	No	Insides of drawers, shelves, and cabinets and exterior cabinet doors as well as countertops.
Yes	No	Bathroom toilets inside/outside, faucets, bathtubs, showers, mirrors and bathroom fans.
Yes	No	Woodwork, trim, baseboards, thermostats, vents, heaters, light switches, outlets, smoke and CO2 detectors, doorbell boxes should all be clean.
Yes	No	Windows inside and out and tracks should be clean.
Yes	No	Hardwood floors and baseboards.
Yes	No	Carpets are stain and damage free
Yes	No	Walls, doors, ceilings are clean and damage free.
Yes	No	Washing/Drying Machine including dryer seal as well as laundry floor and drains.
Yes	No	Garage is clean including walls, floors, and fixtures.

Tenant(s) Signature:	**Date:**
Property Administrator Signature:	**Date:**

Unit #	
Date:	
Inspected By:	

Move In Ready Checklist

Yes	No	Clean Working Light Bulb In Every Socket Including Refrigerator, Oven, Rangehood and Outside Light.
Yes	No	All light fixtures are clean inside and out, including ceiling fans.
Yes	No	Refrigerator and freezer clean, wall behind and floor underneath as well.
Yes	No	Kitchen sink, faucet, sprayer, surround and all countertops including edges and lips should be clean.
Yes	No	Dishwasher should be clean inside and out.
Yes	No	The range, burners, spill pans, inside edges of oven door, and range hood, including range fan filter and light. The floor beneath and the spaces between should be clean.
Yes	No	Kitchen backsplashes, including light and outlet switches, and undersides of all cabinets should be clean.
Yes	No	Insides of drawers, shelves, and cabinets and exterior cabinet doors as well as countertops.
Yes	No	Bathroom toilets inside/outside, faucets, bathtubs, showers, mirrors and bathroom fans.
Yes	No	Woodwork, trim, baseboards, thermostats, vents, heaters, light switches, outlets, smoke and CO2 detectors, doorbell boxes should all be clean.
Yes	No	Windows inside and out and tracks should be clean.
Yes	No	Hardwood floors and baseboards.
Yes	No	Carpets are stain and damage free.
Yes	No	Walls, doors, ceilings are clean and damage free.
Yes	No	Washing/Drying Machine including dryer seal as well as laundry floor and drains.
Yes	No	Garage is clean including walls, floors, and fixtures.

Tenant(s) Signature:	**Date:**
Property Administrator Signature:	**Date:**

Unit #	
Date:	
Inspected By:	

Move In Ready Checklist

Yes	No	Clean Working Light Bulb In Every Socket Including Refrigerator, Oven, Rangehood and Outside Light.
Yes	No	All light fixtures are clean inside and out, including ceiling fans.
Yes	No	Refrigerator and freezer clean, wall behind and floor underneath as well.
Yes	No	Kitchen sink, faucet, sprayer, surround and all countertops including edges and lips should be clean.
Yes	No	Dishwasher should be clean inside and out.
Yes	No	The range, burners, spill pans, inside edges of oven door, and range hood, including range fan filter and light. The floor beneath and the spaces between should be clean.
Yes	No	Kitchen backsplashes, including light and outlet switches, and undersides of all cabinets should be clean.
Yes	No	Insides of drawers, shelves, and cabinets and exterior cabinet doors as well as countertops.
Yes	No	Bathroom toilets inside/outside, faucets, bathtubs, showers, mirrors and bathroom fans.
Yes	No	Woodwork, trim, baseboards, thermostats, vents, heaters, light switches, outlets, smoke and CO2 detectors, doorbell boxes should all be clean.
Yes	No	Windows inside and out and tracks should be clean.
Yes	No	Hardwood floors and baseboards.
Yes	No	Carpets are stain and damage free
Yes	No	Walls, doors, ceilings are clean and damage free.
Yes	No	Washing/Drying Machine including dryer seal as well as laundry floor and drains.
Yes	No	Garage is clean including walls, floors, and fixtures.

Tenant(s) Signature:	**Date:**
Property Administrator Signature:	**Date:**

Unit #	
Date:	
Inspected By:	

Move In Ready Checklist

Yes	No	Clean Working Light Bulb In Every Socket Including Refrigerator, Oven, Rangehood and Outside Light.
Yes	No	All light fixtures are clean inside and out, including ceiling fans.
Yes	No	Refrigerator and freezer clean, wall behind and floor underneath as well.
Yes	No	Kitchen sink, faucet, sprayer, surround and all countertops including edges and lips should be clean.
Yes	No	Dishwasher should be clean inside and out.
Yes	No	The range, burners, spill pans, inside edges of oven door, and range hood, including range fan filter and light. The floor beneath and the spaces between should be clean.
Yes	No	Kitchen backsplashes, including light and outlet switches, and undersides of all cabinets should be clean.
Yes	No	Insides of drawers, shelves, and cabinets and exterior cabinet doors as well as countertops.
Yes	No	Bathroom toilets inside/outside, faucets, bathtubs, showers, mirrors and bathroom fans.
Yes	No	Woodwork, trim, baseboards, thermostats, vents, heaters, light switches, outlets, smoke and CO2 detectors, doorbell boxes should all be clean.
Yes	No	Windows inside and out and tracks should be clean.
Yes	No	Hardwood floors and baseboards.
Yes	No	Carpets are stain and damage free
Yes	No	Walls, doors, ceilings are clean and damage free.
Yes	No	Washing/Drying Machine including dryer seal as well as laundry floor and drains.
Yes	No	Garage is clean including walls, floors, and fixtures.

Tenant(s) Signature:	**Date:**
Property Administrator Signature:	**Date:**

Unit #	
Date:	
Inspected By:	

Move In Ready Checklist

Yes	No	Clean Working Light Bulb In Every Socket Including Refrigerator, Oven, Rangehood and Outside Light.
Yes	No	All light fixtures are clean inside and out, including ceiling fans.
Yes	No	Refrigerator and freezer clean, wall behind and floor underneath as well.
Yes	No	Kitchen sink, faucet, sprayer, surround and all countertops including edges and lips should be clean.
Yes	No	Dishwasher should be clean inside and out.
Yes	No	The range, burners, spill pans, inside edges of oven door, and range hood, including range fan filter and light. The floor beneath and the spaces between should be clean.
Yes	No	Kitchen backsplashes, including light and outlet switches, and undersides of all cabinets should be clean.
Yes	No	Insides of drawers, shelves, and cabinets and exterior cabinet doors as well as countertops.
Yes	No	Bathroom toilets inside/outside, faucets, bathtubs, showers, mirrors and bathroom fans.
Yes	No	Woodwork, trim, baseboards, thermostats, vents, heaters, light switches, outlets, smoke and CO2 detectors, doorbell boxes should all be clean.
Yes	No	Windows inside and out and tracks should be clean.
Yes	No	Hardwood floors and baseboards.
Yes	No	Carpets are stain and damage free
Yes	No	Walls, doors, ceilings are clean and damage free.
Yes	No	Washing/Drying Machine including dryer seal as well as laundry floor and drains.
Yes	No	Garage is clean including walls, floors, and fixtures.

Tenant(s) Signature:	**Date:**
Property Administrator Signature:	**Date:**

Unit #	
Date:	
Inspected By:	

Move In Ready Checklist

Yes	No	Clean Working Light Bulb In Every Socket Including Refrigerator, Oven, Rangehood and Outside Light.
Yes	No	All light fixtures are clean inside and out, including ceiling fans.
Yes	No	Refrigerator and freezer clean, wall behind and floor underneath as well.
Yes	No	Kitchen sink, faucet, sprayer, surround and all countertops including edges and lips should be clean.
Yes	No	Dishwasher should be clean inside and out.
Yes	No	The range, burners, spill pans, inside edges of oven door, and range hood, including range fan filter and light. The floor beneath and the spaces between should be clean.
Yes	No	Kitchen backsplashes, including light and outlet switches, and undersides of all cabinets should be clean.
Yes	No	Insides of drawers, shelves, and cabinets and exterior cabinet doors as well as countertops.
Yes	No	Bathroom toilets inside/outside, faucets, bathtubs, showers, mirrors and bathroom fans.
Yes	No	Woodwork, trim, baseboards, thermostats, vents, heaters, light switches, outlets, smoke and CO2 detectors, doorbell boxes should all be clean.
Yes	No	Windows inside and out and tracks should be clean.
Yes	No	Hardwood floors and baseboards.
Yes	No	Carpets are stain and damage free
Yes	No	Walls, doors, ceilings are clean and damage free.
Yes	No	Washing/Drying Machine including dryer seal as well as laundry floor and drains.
Yes	No	Garage is clean including walls, floors, and fixtures.

Tenant(s) Signature:	**Date:**
Property Administrator Signature:	**Date:**

Unit #	
Date:	
Inspected By:	

Move In Ready Checklist

Yes	No	Clean Working Light Bulb In Every Socket Including Refrigerator, Oven, Rangehood and Outside Light.
Yes	No	All light fixtures are clean inside and out, including ceiling fans.
Yes	No	Refrigerator and freezer clean, wall behind and floor underneath as well.
Yes	No	Kitchen sink, faucet, sprayer, surround and all countertops including edges and lips should be clean.
Yes	No	Dishwasher should be clean inside and out.
Yes	No	The range, burners, spill pans, inside edges of oven door, and range hood, including range fan filter and light. The floor beneath and the spaces between should be clean.
Yes	No	Kitchen backsplashes, including light and outlet switches, and undersides of all cabinets should be clean.
Yes	No	Insides of drawers, shelves, and cabinets and exterior cabinet doors as well as countertops.
Yes	No	Bathroom toilets inside/outside, faucets, bathtubs, showers, mirrors and bathroom fans.
Yes	No	Woodwork, trim, baseboards, thermostats, vents, heaters, light switches, outlets, smoke and CO2 detectors, doorbell boxes should all be clean.
Yes	No	Windows inside and out and tracks should be clean.
Yes	No	Hardwood floors and baseboards.
Yes	No	Carpets are stain and damage free
Yes	No	Walls, doors, ceilings are clean and damage free.
Yes	No	Washing/Drying Machine including dryer seal as well as laundry floor and drains.
Yes	No	Garage is clean including walls, floors, and fixtures.

Tenant(s) Signature:	**Date:**
Property Administrator Signature:	**Date:**

Unit #	
Date:	
Inspected By:	

Move In Ready Checklist

Yes	No	Clean Working Light Bulb In Every Socket Including Refrigerator, Oven, Rangehood and Outside Light.
Yes	No	All light fixtures are clean inside and out, including ceiling fans.
Yes	No	Refrigerator and freezer clean, wall behind and floor underneath as well.
Yes	No	Kitchen sink, faucet, sprayer, surround and all countertops including edges and lips should be clean.
Yes	No	Dishwasher should be clean inside and out.
Yes	No	The range, burners, spill pans, inside edges of oven door, and range hood, including range fan filter and light. The floor beneath and the spaces between should be clean.
Yes	No	Kitchen backsplashes, including light and outlet switches, and undersides of all cabinets should be clean.
Yes	No	Insides of drawers, shelves, and cabinets and exterior cabinet doors as well as countertops.
Yes	No	Bathroom toilets inside/outside, faucets, bathtubs, showers, mirrors and bathroom fans.
Yes	No	Woodwork, trim, baseboards, thermostats, vents, heaters, light switches, outlets, smoke and CO2 detectors, doorbell boxes should all be clean.
Yes	No	Windows inside and out and tracks should be clean.
Yes	No	Hardwood floors and baseboards.
Yes	No	Carpets are stain and damage free
Yes	No	Walls, doors, ceilings are clean and damage free.
Yes	No	Washing/Drying Machine including dryer seal as well as laundry floor and drains.
Yes	No	Garage is clean including walls, floors, and fixtures.

Tenant(s) Signature:	**Date:**
Property Administrator Signature:	**Date:**

Unit #	
Date:	
Inspected By:	

Move In Ready Checklist

Yes	No	Clean Working Light Bulb In Every Socket Including Refrigerator, Oven, Rangehood and Outside Light.
Yes	No	All light fixtures are clean inside and out, including ceiling fans.
Yes	No	Refrigerator and freezer clean, wall behind and floor underneath as well.
Yes	No	Kitchen sink, faucet, sprayer, surround and all countertops including edges and lips should be clean.
Yes	No	Dishwasher should be clean inside and out.
Yes	No	The range, burners, spill pans, inside edges of oven door, and range hood, including range fan filter and light. The floor beneath and the spaces between should be clean.
Yes	No	Kitchen backsplashes, including light and outlet switches, and undersides of all cabinets should be clean.
Yes	No	Insides of drawers, shelves, and cabinets and exterior cabinet doors as well as countertops.
Yes	No	Bathroom toilets inside/outside, faucets, bathtubs, showers, mirrors and bathroom fans.
Yes	No	Woodwork, trim, baseboards, thermostats, vents, heaters, light switches, outlets, smoke and CO2 detectors, doorbell boxes should all be clean.
Yes	No	Windows inside and out and tracks should be clean.
Yes	No	Hardwood floors and baseboards.
Yes	No	Carpets are stain and damage free
Yes	No	Walls, doors, ceilings are clean and damage free.
Yes	No	Washing/Drying Machine including dryer seal as well as laundry floor and drains.
Yes	No	Garage is clean including walls, floors, and fixtures.

Tenant(s) Signature:		**Date:**	
Property Administrator Signature:		**Date:**	

Unit #	
Date:	
Inspected By:	

Move In Ready Checklist

Yes	No	Clean Working Light Bulb In Every Socket Including Refrigerator, Oven, Rangehood and Outside Light.
Yes	No	All light fixtures are clean inside and out, including ceiling fans.
Yes	No	Refrigerator and freezer clean, wall behind and floor underneath as well.
Yes	No	Kitchen sink, faucet, sprayer, surround and all countertops including edges and lips should be clean.
Yes	No	Dishwasher should be clean inside and out.
Yes	No	The range, burners, spill pans, inside edges of oven door, and range hood, including range fan filter and light. The floor beneath and the spaces between should be clean.
Yes	No	Kitchen backsplashes, including light and outlet switches, and undersides of all cabinets should be clean.
Yes	No	Insides of drawers, shelves, and cabinets and exterior cabinet doors as well as countertops.
Yes	No	Bathroom toilets inside/outside, faucets, bathtubs, showers, mirrors and bathroom fans.
Yes	No	Woodwork, trim, baseboards, thermostats, vents, heaters, light switches, outlets, smoke and CO2 detectors, doorbell boxes should all be clean.
Yes	No	Windows inside and out and tracks should be clean.
Yes	No	Hardwood floors and baseboards.
Yes	No	Carpets are stain and damage free
Yes	No	Walls, doors, ceilings are clean and damage free.
Yes	No	Washing/Drying Machine including dryer seal as well as laundry floor and drains.
Yes	No	Garage is clean including walls, floors, and fixtures.

Tenant(s) Signature:	**Date:**
Property Administrator Signature:	**Date:**

Unit #	
Date:	
Inspected By:	

Move In Ready Checklist

Yes	No	Clean Working Light Bulb In Every Socket Including Refrigerator, Oven, Rangehood and Outside Light.
Yes	No	All light fixtures are clean inside and out, including ceiling fans.
Yes	No	Refrigerator and freezer clean, wall behind and floor underneath as well.
Yes	No	Kitchen sink, faucet, sprayer, surround and all countertops including edges and lips should be clean.
Yes	No	Dishwasher should be clean inside and out.
Yes	No	The range, burners, spill pans, inside edges of oven door, and range hood, including range fan filter and light. The floor beneath and the spaces between should be clean.
Yes	No	Kitchen backsplashes, including light and outlet switches, and undersides of all cabinets should be clean.
Yes	No	Insides of drawers, shelves, and cabinets and exterior cabinet doors as well as countertops.
Yes	No	Bathroom toilets inside/outside, faucets, bathtubs, showers, mirrors and bathroom fans.
Yes	No	Woodwork, trim, baseboards, thermostats, vents, heaters, light switches, outlets, smoke and CO2 detectors, doorbell boxes should all be clean.
Yes	No	Windows inside and out and tracks should be clean.
Yes	No	Hardwood floors and baseboards.
Yes	No	Carpets are stain and damage free
Yes	No	Walls, doors, ceilings are clean and damage free.
Yes	No	Washing/Drying Machine including dryer seal as well as laundry floor and drains.
Yes	No	Garage is clean including walls, floors, and fixtures.

Tenant(s) Signature:	**Date:**
Property Administrator Signature:	**Date:**

Unit #	
Date:	
Inspected By:	

Move In Ready Checklist

Yes	No	Clean Working Light Bulb In Every Socket Including Refrigerator, Oven, Rangehood and Outside Light.
Yes	No	All light fixtures are clean inside and out, including ceiling fans.
Yes	No	Refrigerator and freezer clean, wall behind and floor underneath as well.
Yes	No	Kitchen sink, faucet, sprayer, surround and all countertops including edges and lips should be clean.
Yes	No	Dishwasher should be clean inside and out.
Yes	No	The range, burners, spill pans, inside edges of oven door, and range hood, including range fan filter and light. The floor beneath and the spaces between should be clean.
Yes	No	Kitchen backsplashes, including light and outlet switches, and undersides of all cabinets should be clean.
Yes	No	Insides of drawers, shelves, and cabinets and exterior cabinet doors as well as countertops.
Yes	No	Bathroom toilets inside/outside, faucets, bathtubs, showers, mirrors and bathroom fans.
Yes	No	Woodwork, trim, baseboards, thermostats, vents, heaters, light switches, outlets, smoke and CO2 detectors, doorbell boxes should all be clean.
Yes	No	Windows inside and out and tracks should be clean.
Yes	No	Hardwood floors and baseboards.
Yes	No	Carpets are stain and damage free
Yes	No	Walls, doors, ceilings are clean and damage free.
Yes	No	Washing/Drying Machine including dryer seal as well as laundry floor and drains.
Yes	No	Garage is clean including walls, floors, and fixtures.

Tenant(s) Signature:	**Date:**
Property Administrator Signature:	**Date:**

Unit #		
Date:		
Inspected By:		

Move In Ready Checklist

Yes	No	Clean Working Light Bulb In Every Socket Including Refrigerator, Oven, Rangehood and Outside Light.
Yes	No	All light fixtures are clean inside and out, including ceiling fans.
Yes	No	Refrigerator and freezer clean, wall behind and floor underneath as well.
Yes	No	Kitchen sink, faucet, sprayer, surround and all countertops including edges and lips should be clean.
Yes	No	Dishwasher should be clean inside and out.
Yes	No	The range, burners, spill pans, inside edges of oven door, and range hood, including range fan filter and light. The floor beneath and the spaces between should be clean.
Yes	No	Kitchen backsplashes, including light and outlet switches, and undersides of all cabinets should be clean.
Yes	No	Insides of drawers, shelves, and cabinets and exterior cabinet doors as well as countertops.
Yes	No	Bathroom toilets inside/outside, faucets, bathtubs, showers, mirrors and bathroom fans.
Yes	No	Woodwork, trim, baseboards, thermostats, vents, heaters, light switches, outlets, smoke and CO2 detectors, doorbell boxes should all be clean.
Yes	No	Windows inside and out and tracks should be clean.
Yes	No	Hardwood floors and baseboards.
Yes	No	Carpets are stain and damage free
Yes	No	Walls, doors, ceilings are clean and damage free.
Yes	No	Washing/Drying Machine including dryer seal as well as laundry floor and drains.
Yes	No	Garage is clean including walls, floors, and fixtures.

Tenant(s) Signature:	**Date:**
Property Administrator Signature:	**Date:**

Unit #	
Date:	
Inspected By:	

Move In Ready Checklist

Yes	No	Clean Working Light Bulb In Every Socket Including Refrigerator, Oven, Rangehood and Outside Light.
Yes	No	All light fixtures are clean inside and out, including ceiling fans.
Yes	No	Refrigerator and freezer clean, wall behind and floor underneath as well.
Yes	No	Kitchen sink, faucet, sprayer, surround and all countertops including edges and lips should be clean.
Yes	No	Dishwasher should be clean inside and out.
Yes	No	The range, burners, spill pans, inside edges of oven door, and range hood, including range fan filter and light. The floor beneath and the spaces between should be clean.
Yes	No	Kitchen backsplashes, including light and outlet switches, and undersides of all cabinets should be clean.
Yes	No	Insides of drawers, shelves, and cabinets and exterior cabinet doors as well as countertops.
Yes	No	Bathroom toilets inside/outside, faucets, bathtubs, showers, mirrors and bathroom fans.
Yes	No	Woodwork, trim, baseboards, thermostats, vents, heaters, light switches, outlets, smoke and CO2 detectors, doorbell boxes should all be clean.
Yes	No	Windows inside and out and tracks should be clean.
Yes	No	Hardwood floors and baseboards.
Yes	No	Carpets are stain and damage free
Yes	No	Walls, doors, ceilings are clean and damage free.
Yes	No	Washing/Drying Machine including dryer seal as well as laundry floor and drains.
Yes	No	Garage is clean including walls, floors, and fixtures.

Tenant(s) Signature:	**Date:**
Property Administrator Signature: Date:	**Date:**

Unit #	
Date:	
Inspected By:	

Move In Ready Checklist

Yes	No	Clean Working Light Bulb In Every Socket Including Refrigerator, Oven, Rangehood and Outside Light.
Yes	No	All light fixtures are clean inside and out, including ceiling fans.
Yes	No	Refrigerator and freezer clean, wall behind and floor underneath as well.
Yes	No	Kitchen sink, faucet, sprayer, surround and all countertops including edges and lips should be clean.
Yes	No	Dishwasher should be clean inside and out.
Yes	No	The range, burners, spill pans, inside edges of oven door, and range hood, including range fan filter and light. The floor beneath and the spaces between should be clean.
Yes	No	Kitchen backsplashes, including light and outlet switches, and undersides of all cabinets should be clean.
Yes	No	Insides of drawers, shelves, and cabinets and exterior cabinet doors as well as countertops.
Yes	No	Bathroom toilets inside/outside, faucets, bathtubs, showers, mirrors and bathroom fans.
Yes	No	Woodwork, trim, baseboards, thermostats, vents, heaters, light switches, outlets, smoke and CO2 detectors, doorbell boxes should all be clean.
Yes	No	Windows inside and out and tracks should be clean.
Yes	No	Hardwood floors and baseboards.
Yes	No	Carpets are stain and damage free
Yes	No	Walls, doors, ceilings are clean and damage free.
Yes	No	Washing/Drying Machine including dryer seal as well as laundry floor and drains.
Yes	No	Garage is clean including walls, floors, and fixtures.

Tenant(s) Signature:	**Date:**
Property Administrator Signature:	**Date:**

Unit #	
Date:	
Inspected By:	

Move In Ready Checklist

Yes	No	Clean Working Light Bulb In Every Socket Including Refrigerator, Oven, Rangehood and Outside Light.
Yes	No	All light fixtures are clean inside and out, including ceiling fans.
Yes	No	Refrigerator and freezer clean, wall behind and floor underneath as well.
Yes	No	Kitchen sink, faucet, sprayer, surround and all countertops including edges and lips should be clean.
Yes	No	Dishwasher should be clean inside and out.
Yes	No	The range, burners, spill pans, inside edges of oven door, and range hood, including range fan filter and light. The floor beneath and the spaces between should be clean.
Yes	No	Kitchen backsplashes, including light and outlet switches, and undersides of all cabinets should be clean.
Yes	No	Insides of drawers, shelves, and cabinets and exterior cabinet doors as well as countertops.
Yes	No	Bathroom toilets inside/outside, faucets, bathtubs, showers, mirrors and bathroom fans.
Yes	No	Woodwork, trim, baseboards, thermostats, vents, heaters, light switches, outlets, smoke and CO2 detectors, doorbell boxes should all be clean.
Yes	No	Windows inside and out and tracks should be clean.
Yes	No	Hardwood floors and baseboards.
Yes	No	Carpets are stain and damage free
Yes	No	Walls, doors, ceilings are clean and damage free.
Yes	No	Washing/Drying Machine including dryer seal as well as laundry floor and drains.
Yes	No	Garage is clean including walls, floors, and fixtures.

Tenant(s) Signature:	**Date:**
Property Administrator Signature:	**Date:**

Unit #	
Date:	
Inspected By:	

Move In Ready Checklist

Yes	No	Clean Working Light Bulb In Every Socket Including Refrigerator, Oven, Rangehood and Outside Light.
Yes	No	All light fixtures are clean inside and out, including ceiling fans.
Yes	No	Refrigerator and freezer clean, wall behind and floor underneath as well.
Yes	No	Kitchen sink, faucet, sprayer, surround and all countertops including edges and lips should be clean.
Yes	No	Dishwasher should be clean inside and out.
Yes	No	The range, burners, spill pans, inside edges of oven door, and range hood, including range fan filter and light. The floor beneath and the spaces between should be clean.
Yes	No	Kitchen backsplashes, including light and outlet switches, and undersides of all cabinets should be clean.
Yes	No	Insides of drawers, shelves, and cabinets and exterior cabinet doors as well as countertops.
Yes	No	Bathroom toilets inside/outside, faucets, bathtubs, showers, mirrors and bathroom fans.
Yes	No	Woodwork, trim, baseboards, thermostats, vents, heaters, light switches, outlets, smoke and CO2 detectors, doorbell boxes should all be clean.
Yes	No	Windows inside and out and tracks should be clean.
Yes	No	Hardwood floors and baseboards.
Yes	No	Carpets are stain and damage free
Yes	No	Walls, doors, ceilings are clean and damage free.
Yes	No	Washing/Drying Machine including dryer seal as well as laundry floor and drains.
Yes	No	Garage is clean including walls, floors, and fixtures.

Tenant(s) Signature:	**Date:**
Property Administrator Signature:	**Date:**

Unit #	
Date:	
Inspected By:	

Move In Ready Checklist

Yes	No	Clean Working Light Bulb In Every Socket Including Refrigerator, Oven, Rangehood and Outside Light.
Yes	No	All light fixtures are clean inside and out, including ceiling fans.
Yes	No	Refrigerator and freezer clean, wall behind and floor underneath as well.
Yes	No	Kitchen sink, faucet, sprayer, surround and all countertops including edges and lips should be clean.
Yes	No	Dishwasher should be clean inside and out.
Yes	No	The range, burners, spill pans, inside edges of oven door, and range hood, including range fan filter and light. The floor beneath and the spaces between should be clean.
Yes	No	Kitchen backsplashes, including light and outlet switches, and undersides of all cabinets should be clean.
Yes	No	Insides of drawers, shelves, and cabinets and exterior cabinet doors as well as countertops.
Yes	No	Bathroom toilets inside/outside, faucets, bathtubs, showers, mirrors and bathroom fans.
Yes	No	Woodwork, trim, baseboards, thermostats, vents, heaters, light switches, outlets, smoke and CO2 detectors, doorbell boxes should all be clean.
Yes	No	Windows inside and out and tracks should be clean.
Yes	No	Hardwood floors and baseboards.
Yes	No	Carpets are stain and damage free
Yes	No	Walls, doors, ceilings are clean and damage free.
Yes	No	Washing/Drying Machine including dryer seal as well as laundry floor and drains.
Yes	No	Garage is clean including walls, floors, and fixtures.

Tenant(s) Signature:	**Date:**
Property Administrator Signature:	**Date:**

Unit #	
Date:	
Inspected By:	

Move In Ready Checklist

Yes	No	Clean Working Light Bulb In Every Socket Including Refrigerator, Oven, Rangehood and Outside Light.
Yes	No	All light fixtures are clean inside and out, including ceiling fans.
Yes	No	Refrigerator and freezer clean, wall behind and floor underneath as well.
Yes	No	Kitchen sink, faucet, sprayer, surround and all countertops including edges and lips should be clean.
Yes	No	Dishwasher should be clean inside and out.
Yes	No	The range, burners, spill pans, inside edges of oven door, and range hood, including range fan filter and light. The floor beneath and the spaces between should be clean.
Yes	No	Kitchen backsplashes, including light and outlet switches, and undersides of all cabinets should be clean.
Yes	No	Insides of drawers, shelves, and cabinets and exterior cabinet doors as well as countertops.
Yes	No	Bathroom toilets inside/outside, faucets, bathtubs, showers, mirrors and bathroom fans.
Yes	No	Woodwork, trim, baseboards, thermostats, vents, heaters, light switches, outlets, smoke and CO2 detectors, doorbell boxes should all be clean.
Yes	No	Windows inside and out and tracks should be clean.
Yes	No	Hardwood floors and baseboards.
Yes	No	Carpets are stain and damage free
Yes	No	Walls, doors, ceilings are clean and damage free.
Yes	No	Washing/Drying Machine including dryer seal as well as laundry floor and drains.
Yes	No	Garage is clean including walls, floors, and fixtures.

Tenant(s) Signature:	**Date:**
Property Administrator Signature:	**Date:**

Unit #	
Date:	
Inspected By:	

Move In Ready Checklist

Yes	No	Clean Working Light Bulb In Every Socket Including Refrigerator, Oven, Rangehood and Outside Light.
Yes	No	All light fixtures are clean inside and out, including ceiling fans.
Yes	No	Refrigerator and freezer clean, wall behind and floor underneath as well.
Yes	No	Kitchen sink, faucet, sprayer, surround and all countertops including edges and lips should be clean.
Yes	No	Dishwasher should be clean inside and out.
Yes	No	The range, burners, spill pans, inside edges of oven door, and range hood, including range fan filter and light. The floor beneath and the spaces between should be clean.
Yes	No	Kitchen backsplashes, including light and outlet switches, and undersides of all cabinets should be clean.
Yes	No	Insides of drawers, shelves, and cabinets and exterior cabinet doors as well as countertops.
Yes	No	Bathroom toilets inside/outside, faucets, bathtubs, showers, mirrors and bathroom fans.
Yes	No	Woodwork, trim, baseboards, thermostats, vents, heaters, light switches, outlets, smoke and CO2 detectors, doorbell boxes should all be clean.
Yes	No	Windows inside and out and tracks should be clean.
Yes	No	Hardwood floors and baseboards.
Yes	No	Carpets are stain and damage free
Yes	No	Walls, doors, ceilings are clean and damage free.
Yes	No	Washing/Drying Machine including dryer seal as well as laundry floor and drains.
Yes	No	Garage is clean including walls, floors, and fixtures.

Tenant(s) Signature:	**Date:**
Property Administrator Signature:	**Date:**

Unit #	
Date:	
Inspected By:	

Move In Ready Checklist

Yes	No	Clean Working Light Bulb In Every Socket Including Refrigerator, Oven, Rangehood and Outside Light.
Yes	No	All light fixtures are clean inside and out, including ceiling fans.
Yes	No	Refrigerator and freezer clean, wall behind and floor underneath as well.
Yes	No	Kitchen sink, faucet, sprayer, surround and all countertops including edges and lips should be clean.
Yes	No	Dishwasher should be clean inside and out.
Yes	No	The range, burners, spill pans, inside edges of oven door, and range hood, including range fan filter and light. The floor beneath and the spaces between should be clean.
Yes	No	Kitchen backsplashes, including light and outlet switches, and undersides of all cabinets should be clean.
Yes	No	Insides of drawers, shelves, and cabinets and exterior cabinet doors as well as countertops.
Yes	No	Bathroom toilets inside/outside, faucets, bathtubs, showers, mirrors and bathroom fans.
Yes	No	Woodwork, trim, baseboards, thermostats, vents, heaters, light switches, outlets, smoke and CO2 detectors, doorbell boxes should all be clean.
Yes	No	Windows inside and out and tracks should be clean.
Yes	No	Hardwood floors and baseboards.
Yes	No	Carpets are stain and damage free
Yes	No	Walls, doors, ceilings are clean and damage free.
Yes	No	Washing/Drying Machine including dryer seal as well as laundry floor and drains.
Yes	No	Garage is clean including walls, floors, and fixtures.

Tenant(s) Signature:	**Date:**
Property Administrator Signature:	**Date:**

Unit #	
Date:	
Inspected By:	

Move In Ready Checklist

Yes	No	Clean Working Light Bulb In Every Socket Including Refrigerator, Oven, Rangehood and Outside Light.
Yes	No	All light fixtures are clean inside and out, including ceiling fans.
Yes	No	Refrigerator and freezer clean, wall behind and floor underneath as well.
Yes	No	Kitchen sink, faucet, sprayer, surround and all countertops including edges and lips should be clean.
Yes	No	Dishwasher should be clean inside and out.
Yes	No	The range, burners, spill pans, inside edges of oven door, and range hood, including range fan filter and light. The floor beneath and the spaces between should be clean.
Yes	No	Kitchen backsplashes, including light and outlet switches, and undersides of all cabinets should be clean.
Yes	No	Insides of drawers, shelves, and cabinets and exterior cabinet doors as well as countertops.
Yes	No	Bathroom toilets inside/outside, faucets, bathtubs, showers, mirrors and bathroom fans.
Yes	No	Woodwork, trim, baseboards, thermostats, vents, heaters, light switches, outlets, smoke and CO2 detectors, doorbell boxes should all be clean.
Yes	No	Windows inside and out and tracks should be clean.
Yes	No	Hardwood floors and baseboards.
Yes	No	Carpets are stain and damage free
Yes	No	Walls, doors, ceilings are clean and damage free.
Yes	No	Washing/Drying Machine including dryer seal as well as laundry floor and drains.
Yes	No	Garage is clean including walls, floors, and fixtures.

Tenant(s) Signature:	**Date:**
Property Administrator Signature:	**Date:**

Unit #	
Date:	
Inspected By:	

Move In Ready Checklist

Yes	No	Clean Working Light Bulb In Every Socket Including Refrigerator, Oven, Rangehood and Outside Light.
Yes	No	All light fixtures are clean inside and out, including ceiling fans.
Yes	No	Refrigerator and freezer clean, wall behind and floor underneath as well.
Yes	No	Kitchen sink, faucet, sprayer, surround and all countertops including edges and lips should be clean.
Yes	No	Dishwasher should be clean inside and out.
Yes	No	The range, burners, spill pans, inside edges of oven door, and range hood, including range fan filter and light. The floor beneath and the spaces between should be clean.
Yes	No	Kitchen backsplashes, including light and outlet switches, and undersides of all cabinets should be clean.
Yes	No	Insides of drawers, shelves, and cabinets and exterior cabinet doors as well as countertops.
Yes	No	Bathroom toilets inside/outside, faucets, bathtubs, showers, mirrors and bathroom fans.
Yes	No	Woodwork, trim, baseboards, thermostats, vents, heaters, light switches, outlets, smoke and CO2 detectors, doorbell boxes should all be clean.
Yes	No	Windows inside and out and tracks should be clean.
Yes	No	Hardwood floors and baseboards.
Yes	No	Carpets are stain and damage free
Yes	No	Walls, doors, ceilings are clean and damage free.
Yes	No	Washing/Drying Machine including dryer seal as well as laundry floor and drains.
Yes	No	Garage is clean including walls, floors, and fixtures.

Tenant(s) Signature:	**Date:**
Property Administrator Signature:	**Date:**

Unit #	
Date:	
Inspected By:	

Move In Ready Checklist

Yes	No	Clean Working Light Bulb In Every Socket Including Refrigerator, Oven, Rangehood and Outside Light.
Yes	No	All light fixtures are clean inside and out, including ceiling fans.
Yes	No	Refrigerator and freezer clean, wall behind and floor underneath as well.
Yes	No	Kitchen sink, faucet, sprayer, surround and all countertops including edges and lips should be clean.
Yes	No	Dishwasher should be clean inside and out.
Yes	No	The range, burners, spill pans, inside edges of oven door, and range hood, including range fan filter and light. The floor beneath and the spaces between should be clean.
Yes	No	Kitchen backsplashes, including light and outlet switches, and undersides of all cabinets should be clean.
Yes	No	Insides of drawers, shelves, and cabinets and exterior cabinet doors as well as countertops.
Yes	No	Bathroom toilets inside/outside, faucets, bathtubs, showers, mirrors and bathroom fans.
Yes	No	Woodwork, trim, baseboards, thermostats, vents, heaters, light switches, outlets, smoke and CO2 detectors, doorbell boxes should all be clean.
Yes	No	Windows inside and out and tracks should be clean.
Yes	No	Hardwood floors and baseboards.
Yes	No	Carpets are stain and damage free
Yes	No	Walls, doors, ceilings are clean and damage free.
Yes	No	Washing/Drying Machine including dryer seal as well as laundry floor and drains.
Yes	No	Garage is clean including walls, floors, and fixtures.

Tenant(s) Signature: **Date:**

Property Administrator Signature: **Date:**

Unit #	
Date:	
Inspected By:	

Move In Ready Checklist

Yes	No	Clean Working Light Bulb In Every Socket Including Refrigerator, Oven, Rangehood and Outside Light.
Yes	No	All light fixtures are clean inside and out, including ceiling fans.
Yes	No	Refrigerator and freezer clean, wall behind and floor underneath as well.
Yes	No	Kitchen sink, faucet, sprayer, surround and all countertops including edges and lips should be clean.
Yes	No	Dishwasher should be clean inside and out.
Yes	No	The range, burners, spill pans, inside edges of oven door, and range hood, including range fan filter and light. The floor beneath and the spaces between should be clean.
Yes	No	Kitchen backsplashes, including light and outlet switches, and undersides of all cabinets should be clean.
Yes	No	Insides of drawers, shelves, and cabinets and exterior cabinet doors as well as countertops.
Yes	No	Bathroom toilets inside/outside, faucets, bathtubs, showers, mirrors and bathroom fans.
Yes	No	Woodwork, trim, baseboards, thermostats, vents, heaters, light switches, outlets, smoke and CO2 detectors, doorbell boxes should all be clean.
Yes	No	Windows inside and out and tracks should be clean.
Yes	No	Hardwood floors and baseboards.
Yes	No	Carpets are stain and damage free
Yes	No	Walls, doors, ceilings are clean and damage free.
Yes	No	Washing/Drying Machine including dryer seal as well as laundry floor and drains.
Yes	No	Garage is clean including walls, floors, and fixtures.

Tenant(s) Signature:	**Date:**
Property Administrator Signature:	**Date:**

Unit #:	
Date:	
Inspected By:	

Move In Ready Checklist

Yes	No	Clean Working Light Bulb In Every Socket Including Refrigerator, Oven, Rangehood and Outside Light.
Yes	No	All light fixtures are clean inside and out, including ceiling fans.
Yes	No	Refrigerator and freezer clean, wall behind and floor underneath as well.
Yes	No	Kitchen sink, faucet, sprayer, surround and all countertops including edges and lips should be clean.
Yes	No	Dishwasher should be clean inside and out.
Yes	No	The range, burners, spill pans, inside edges of oven door, and range hood, including range fan filter and light. The floor beneath and the spaces between should be clean.
Yes	No	Kitchen backsplashes, including light and outlet switches, and undersides of all cabinets should be clean.
Yes	No	Insides of drawers, shelves, and cabinets and exterior cabinet doors as well as countertops.
Yes	No	Bathroom toilets inside/outside, faucets, bathtubs, showers, mirrors and bathroom fans.
Yes	No	Woodwork, trim, baseboards, thermostats, vents, heaters, light switches, outlets, smoke and CO2 detectors, doorbell boxes should all be clean.
Yes	No	Windows inside and out and tracks should be clean.
Yes	No	Hardwood floors and baseboards.
Yes	No	Carpets are stain and damage free
Yes	No	Walls, doors, ceilings are clean and damage free.
Yes	No	Washing/Drying Machine including dryer seal as well as laundry floor and drains.
Yes	No	Garage is clean including walls, floors, and fixtures.

Tenant(s) Signature: **Date:**

Property Administrator Signature: **Date:**

www.ingramcontent.com/pod-product-compliance
Lightning Source LLC
Chambersburg PA
CBHW081701220526
45466CB00009B/2845